The Inventors

The Inventors

Nobel Prizes in Chemistry, Physics, and Medicine

by Nathan Aaseng

Lerner Publications Company • Minneapolis

To Bill Watson and family

The publisher wishes to thank Anthony D. Boucher
and John P. Enright for their assistance in the
preparation of this book.

Diagrams by Laura Westlund

The glossary on page 75 gives definitions for the
words in bold face type.

LIBRARY OF CONGRESS CATALOGING-IN-PUBLICATION DATA

Aaseng, Nathan.
  The inventors.

  (Nobel Prize winners)
  Includes index.
  Summary: Discusses eight inventions or discoveries
(X ray, radio, EKG, phase contrast microscope, transistor,
radiocarbon dating, laser, and CT scan) which brought the
Nobel prize to their developers.
  1. Inventions—Juvenile literature. 2. Nobel prizes—Juvenile
literature. [1. Inventions. 2. Nobel prizes] I. Title. II. Series.
T48.A27   1988   609   87-3979
ISBN 0-8225-0651-3 (lib. bdg.)

Manufactured in the United States of America

1 2 3 4 5 6 7 8 9 10 97 96 95 94 93 92 91 90 89 88

Contents

Alfred Nobel's laboratory

Introduction

Deep in the musty, cobwebbed cellar of an ancient stone mansion, the mad scientist pores over pages of scribbled notes. An eccentric hermit who cares nothing for people or society, he wades through a forest of test tubes, wires, switches, motors, boxes full of tools, crates of scrap iron, and cages of white mice in order to lock the door of his laboratory. Far into the night, the mansion trembles from the jolt of electric bursts and the rumbling of explosions, and the reek of burnt sulfur filters out through cracks in the door. The inventor is unlocking a secret of the universe.

It may be that Swedish inventor Alfred Nobel did as much as anyone to create that image of the mysterious inventor-scientist. Carrying on the family tradition of perfecting and manufacturing explosives, Nobel performed dangerous experiments. In 1864, an accident with the unstable substance nitroglycerin shattered the Nobel laboratory in Stockholm and killed several people, including Alfred's youngest brother. Frightened officials then banned all experiments with nitroglycerin within the city, and Alfred Nobel was forced to carry on his work on a barge in the middle of a lake outside the city limits.

Within this floating fortress, which must have seemed a factory of terror to the common folk who dared venture close enough to see it, Nobel made his greatest discovery. In 1867, the secretive Nobel patented an invention that used the power of nitroglycerin to set off enormous explosions. He called this new material dynamite, and it quickly made him one of the richest men in the world. But although dynamite proved to be a very useful tool for industry, it could also cause death and destruction beyond anything the world had ever known. The image of the mad inventor had reached new heights.

Nobel, who never married and rarely appeared in public, remained a lonely, puzzling figure until his death in 1896. His influence on inventors and inventions, however, was far from over. Guilt-ridden because of the suffering caused by his invention, he used some of his fortune to set up the Nobel Prizes: five cash awards to be given each year to those who have done the most to benefit humanity in the areas of physiology or medicine, physics, chemistry, and literature, or by furthering world peace.

One can't help but notice that the business of inventing has changed drastically since the days of Alfred Nobel. As early as 1899, the director of the United States Patent Office declared that "everything that can be invented has been invented." While that remark has proved to be laughable, it probably is true that there aren't many earth-shattering discoveries that a person can make without help anymore. As some scientists have put it, all the "easy" things have been invented. The days of ticking off a list of inventions and giving the readily identifiable name of the inventor of each one are fading fast. The lone inventor has gradually been replaced by groups of highly trained scientists who require massive funding and build upon the ideas and discoveries of previous research teams.

The evolution of invention in the 20th century can be traced in the progression of this book, which tells the story of eight inventions whose creators were honored

The Nobel medals for physics, chemistry, and physiology or medicine. Alfred Nobel appears on the front of all three medals (center). The reverse sides of the medals for physics and chemistry (left), which are identical, show the Genius of Science standing next to a goddess who represents nature. The reverse side of the medal for physiology or medicine (right) shows the Genius of Medicine drawing water for a sick girl.

with the Nobel Prize in chemistry, physics, or physiology or medicine. Some of the prizewinners—including Wilhelm Roentgen (X ray), Guglielmo Marconi (radio), and even one of the more recent Nobel laureates, Godfrey Hounsfield (CT scanner)—fit the stereotypical image of the inventor in that they basically worked alone in laboratories in their own homes. Others—such as the research team of William Shockley, John Bardeen, and Walter Brattain (transistor), who were financed by a corporation—represent the new direction that inventing is taking.

The new corporate nature of research has made the job of the Nobel awards committee enormously difficult. After a prize has been awarded for one year, it takes the judges most of the next twelve months to evaluate the nominations for the following year. The process becomes even more difficult and time-consuming when there have been many stages in the development of an important invention or discovery. For example, the prize for the laser was awarded to several people whose ideas led to the instrument's development rather than being awarded to Dr. Theodore Maiman, who actually produced the world's first laser.

The image of the mad scientist will probably never fade as long as new discoveries are used for purposes of destruction. But the inventions described in this book can genuinely claim to have provided enormous benefits to all of us. Some of these inventions eliminate pain

Alfred Nobel

and save lives while giving us knowledge about ourselves. Others tell us about our planet and its very beginnings. Still others help us to organize and analyze the information we have gathered so it can be used today and then stored for future generations.

It is possible, decades from now, that one or more of these inventions may prove to be the cornerstone of an even greater invention—one that will change the world in ways that we cannot yet imagine. Such was Alfred Nobel's hope, which continues to live in the results of his last will and testament: the Nobel Prizes.

1

X-ray Photography: Seeing Past the Skin

The human body may be an exquisite piece of machinery many notches above clocks, automobile engines, and refrigerators, but when it comes to repairs, its design is not ideal. For most of human existence, there wasn't much chance for survival when something went wrong with the inner workings of the body. Unlike lesser machines that could be opened up, examined, and repaired without any fuss, the only way to get past the outer layers of flesh to see what was malfunctioning involved unbearable pain and a good deal of risk with no guarantee that any good would come from all that suffering.

The three medical inventions discussed in this book have probably done more than anything else to make the human body a readily repairable apparatus. The first of these, Wilhelm Roentgen's X ray, so impressed the scientific community that in 1901 Roentgen was awarded the first Nobel Prize for physics, receiving 17 of the 29 nominations.

As has happened so often in scientific breakthroughs, the discovery of the X ray was simply a matter of a bright person being in the right place at the right time. The person was a 50-year-old German physics professor known for his honesty and selfless devotion to research. The place was a small laboratory that was, as expected of a typical scientist-inventor, located underneath his residence. The

X rays have been especially valuable to the world of medicine. Here a technician examines a chest X ray.

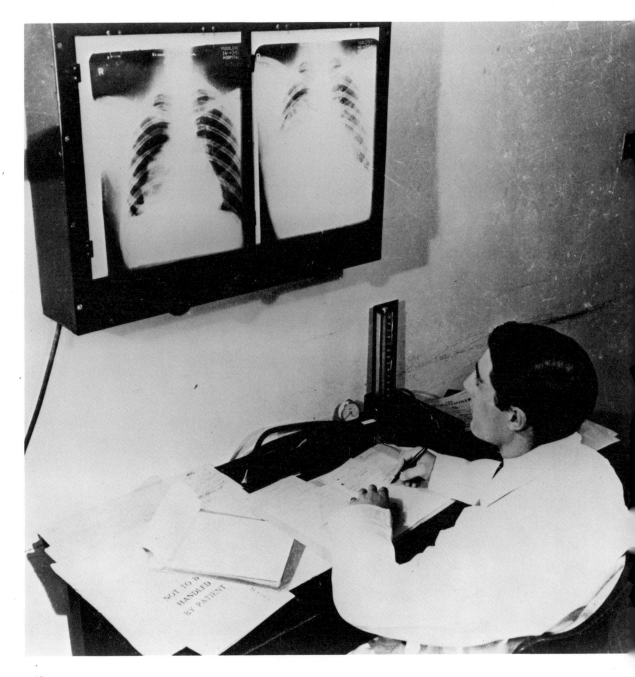

time, again according to script, was well past normal bedtime hours on the night of November 8, 1895.

Ruined Plates

On that November evening, Wilhelm Roentgen, who was continually looking for a new area of physics to explore, had turned his attention to the study of the Crookes tube. This was a glass cylinder with the air pumped out of it through which an electric **current** was passed. Scientists who had worked with the Crookes tube had observed that when the electric current was turned on, a greenish glow radiated from the tube. Roentgen wanted to know more about these curious rays.

Roentgen discovered X rays in this laboratory at his home in Würzburg, Germany.

Roentgen's first experiment with the rays was to see if black paper could block them the way it blocked normal light. He made sure his laboratory was completely dark and then covered the Crookes tube with a black cardboard box. When the current was turned on, the room remained dark except for a green glow several feet from the box. The light was coming from a cardboard screen treated with a chemical that glowed when exposed to light. Roentgen knew he was not dealing with ordinary light when he realized that the rays must have passed through the box to get to the screen. Working in silence and secrecy, he set out to discover everything he could about these rays, which he called X rays because x is the mathematical symbol for the unknown.

One irritating feature of X rays was their ability to ruin perfectly good photographic plates. These plates were the "film" used in cameras at the turn of the century. When exposed to the rays, the plates would fog over. This information was hardly worth noticing (after all, ordinary light did the same thing) until Roentgen found that it wasn't even safe to keep plates in the same room as the X rays. When he reached into his desk for a plate that had been kept in a drawer away from the rays, Roentgen discovered that it too had fogged up.

Instead of throwing the plate away in disgust, however, Roentgen took the time to develop it. So it was quite by accident that he discovered the perfectly etched

Wilhelm Roentgen

image of a key on the photographic plate. Although it appeared to be magic, Roentgen kept his head and looked for an explanation. There hadn't been a key in the drawer—of that he was certain—but he had left a key on top of the desk. The only explanation, therefore, was that the rays had gone through the wooden desk top to get to the plate but had been partially blocked by the metal key.

Death Rays

More experiments followed in which Roentgen tried to find a material that would completely block these mysterious rays. After watching X rays penetrate a wide range of materials—from paper to cloth to wood and even metal—the scientist discovered that they had finally met their match in one heavy metal: lead.

Conscientiously following up on his observations, Roentgen set up a screen that was sensitive to the rays a short distance from the Crookes tube and turned on the electricity. Then he picked up a small disk made of lead and held it between the screen and the tube. Turning to observe the screen, Roentgen saw what he had expected to see: the precise outline of the disk where it was blocking the rays. But that sight was overshadowed by the stunning image of the bones of

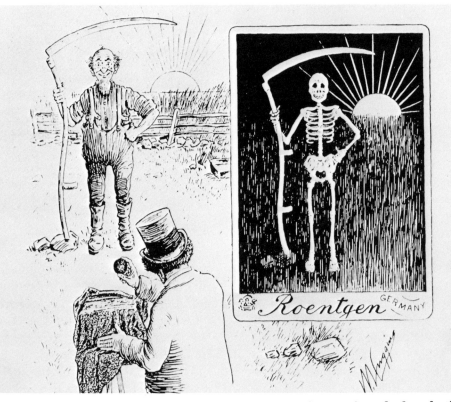

In this cartoon of "the new Roentgen photography," the farmer is asked to look pleasant for his X ray.

his own finger and thumb, which appeared on the screen just as if all the flesh had fallen away. The X rays were passing through his hand, leaving shadows where the bones were.

Roentgen worked more feverishly than ever, spending weeks in the laboratory documenting his astounding discovery. After organizing all his observations and developing enough X-ray photographs to prove his discovery, Roentgen was finally ready to share his secret with the rest of the world, starting with his own wife.

When Bertha Roentgen saw her hand reduced to bones on the X-ray screen, she was convinced that it was a bad omen that meant she was soon to die. Mrs. Roentgen's was not the only extreme reaction to this strange new ray. There were doomsayers who claimed that Roentgen had stumbled upon death rays that would soon destroy humanity. Others painted far brighter, if equally ridiculous, pictures. There were claims that X rays could make blind people see and turn ordinary metals into gold. Temperance groups welcomed the X ray as their ultimate weapon; they were convinced that it was a tool that would wipe out drinking and smoking by showing in graphic detail how these vices destroyed the organs of the body. Perhaps the most ambitious design for X rays was an experiment in which a researcher tried to show that students could be taught anatomy by having diagrams beamed by X ray right into their brains!

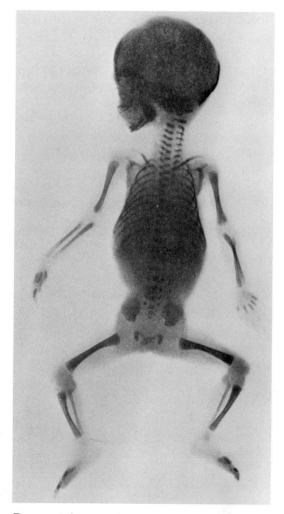

Roentgen's new invention gave doctors a look at the bone structure of a five-month-old fetus in this X ray taken in 1904.

Fortunately, the reaction of the medical world was far more sane. Following Roentgen's instructions, hospitals immediately began to use X rays to diagnose

15

problems in the human body. Within five years, nearly every hospital in the Western world used X rays for such procedures as locating bullets, detecting foreign objects that had been swallowed, and helping to set breaks in bones.

Roentgen left the further exploration of X rays to other scientists, and within a couple of decades, the nature of what we continue to call X rays became well documented. We now know that X rays are related to visible light, the same light you see every day. They are both forms of **radiation** and they both move in waves, but X rays have much shorter **wavelengths**—or distances between the tops of their waves—than does visible light. Their short wavelengths (less than 1/10,000 those of visible light) enable X rays to pass through most materials.

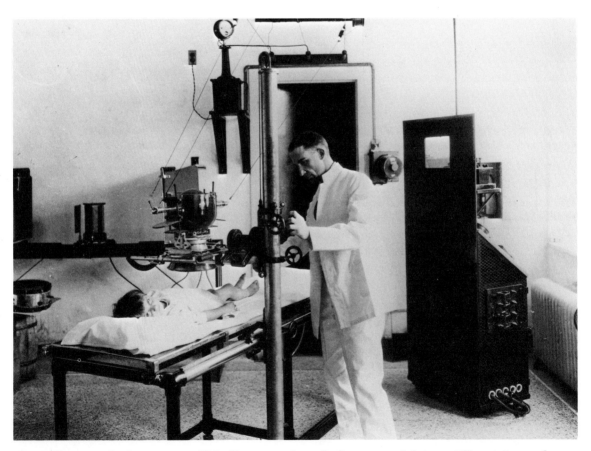

Once Roentgen had announced his discovery, hospitals were quick to put X rays to work.

The denser the material, however, the fewer the rays that can get through and the darker the shadow that appears. This is why bones, which are far denser than their surrounding flesh, show up as shadows on an X ray.

X rays Today

Today, more than 200 million X-ray photographs are taken every year to help identify and correct health problems. They are especially valuable for diagnosing lung cancer because the differences in the densities of the tissues in the chest show up clearly on an X ray. X rays are now routinely used, not only by physicians, but also by chiropractors for detecting spinal misalignments and by dentists for locating small cavities. Industry uses X rays to inspect welds and to detect flaws and weak spots in pipes, insulation, high-pressure boilers, and other equipment. Even the art world, which uses X rays to help identify old paintings, has profited from Roentgen's discovery.

As with most discoveries, X rays haven't proven to be all good. Due to the early lack of information about this radiation, many scientists and patients at one time suffered illness as a result of prolonged exposure to the rays. The penetrating X ray, it was found, can damage cells and produce cancer. But once such precautions as limiting exposure times and using lead as a protective shield were begun, X rays could be used more safely.

Although X rays have not been able to turn metal into gold, nor beam knowledge into the brains of students, their many uses have made the selection of Wilhelm Roentgen as the first Nobel Prize winner for physics an acclaimed decision.

By the 1930s, radio had become an important source of news and entertainment. These portable radios were displayed at the Northwest Radio Show in 1937.

2

The Radio:
Messages Through the Air

If Guglielmo Marconi were a teenager today, he could easily be a computer hacker. Spurred on by a burning curiosity and wielding tremendous powers of concentration, he might even stumble on to top-secret information that could get him into trouble. Although this is sheer speculation, it illustrates the type of person who first brought long-range wireless communication to the world.

Marconi was a 20-year-old amateur scientist experimenting on his own when he began working on an invention that would usher in the modern age of rapid communication. What he called the wireless telegraph, or wireless, we know today as the radio. Marconi's feat of winning the 1909 Nobel Prize for physics, one of the most prestigious awards in science, was an amazing accomplishment for a young man who had never even attended college.

Marconi's idea that messages could be sent through the air was not a sudden flash of brilliance that came out of nowhere. The groundwork for wireless communication was laid as far back as the early 1800s when Englishman Michael Faraday and Joseph Henry from the United States both discovered that an electric current could somehow jump from one wire to another, even when the two wires were not touching. While this observation may not sound very important in itself, it was the first in a series of discoveries that led to the development of the radio.

Scottish physicist James Clerk Maxwell took Henry and Faraday's discovery a step further when he theorized how the current traveled from one wire to the other. In his *Treatise on Electricity and Magnetism,*

Michael Faraday helped lay the ground-work for wireless communication.

published in 1873, Maxwell suggested that an electric current, such as the one that was sent up the first wire, creates an area of force in the air called a **magnetic field**. That magnetic field creates another magnetic field, which, in turn, creates another one, and so on—much the same way a rock dropped into water creates an ever-widening circle of ripples. This chain of magnetic fields travels through the air until it touches something that can **conduct**, or transmit, an electric current, such as another wire. Maxwell called the chain of magnetic fields **electromagnetic waves**. Fifteen years later, the German scientist Heinrich Hertz showed that Maxwell's ideas were more than just impressive formulas when he made a spark of electricity jump across a room from one coil of wire—the **transmitter**—to another—the **receiver**.

Despite his youth and relative lack of training in physics, Marconi was able to see what many experienced scientists had missed: there was a practical application for the newly discovered electromagnetic waves. In the late 1800s, long-range communication was provided by the telegraph, which could send electric **signals** in Morse code through wires from one operator to another. But the use of the telegraph was limited because the sender and the receiver had to be connected by a telegraph wire.

In the tiny spark that jumped across the room in Hertz's experiments with electromagnetic waves, Marconi saw the potential for the elimination of the need for a wire to transmit electric signals. This would make it possible for ships to communicate with shore and with each other, possibly saving lives in a storm. It would also allow governments to communicate with their armies and their diplomats in distant lands. Geographical barriers would no longer prevent people from communicating with each other.

Experiments at Home

Guglielmo Marconi had both the fortune and misfortune of being born into a wealthy Italian family. His father provided him with the financial backing for his experiments, but constantly harassed him as a good-for-nothing freeloader. Marconi, however, had his mother's support and the determination to make his ideas work.

Marconi was tutored at home until age 12. As a teenager, he attended the Leghorn Technical Institute, where he became so fascinated with physics and chemistry that he took private lessons in science. Marconi's formal schooling ended when he failed the entrance examination for the University of Bologna, and he had to continue his education on his own. Fortunately for Marconi, a neighbor who was a professor at the university arranged for him to use some of the university facilities, including the library. Always tinkering with some homemade physics experiment in a laboratory that he had put together in his attic, Marconi learned countless lessons through trial and error. One of the most

Guglielmo Marconi

serious errors involved cutting off a piece of his finger while constructing his own crude transmitter.

After reading a journal account in 1894 of Heinrich Hertz's work with electromagnetic waves, Marconi became obsessed with the notion that Hertz's waves could make wireless telegraphy possible. He realized that in order for the waves to have any use as a communication device, they would have to travel greater distances than just across a room. Ignoring his father's scoldings, Marconi immersed himself in his experiments in his attic laboratory.

The basic problem, as Marconi saw it, was how to improve the two ends of the operation: the transmitting power and the receiving sensitivity. Gradually, Marconi found ways to increase his power and discovered that he could send electric signals across the room to move a compass point. Better yet, he rigged up an apparatus that would send out a signal from his top-floor lab that could ring a bell on the ground floor.

As for the receiver, Marconi was dissatisfied with the commonly used design in which the electromagnetic waves were "caught" by metal filings in a tube. This receiving procedure was called the coherer method because the particles clumped together—or cohered—and stayed that way even after the signal was over. Once Marconi had rigged up an apparatus that tapped the coherer and separated the particles after each transmission, it was possible to send a series of uninterrupted signals. This was crucial in the sending of any code.

Stretching the Limits

When his system outgrew the house, Marconi moved outdoors. One of the ways he had found to increase the wavelength—and, therefore, the strength— of the signal was to place metal plates on either side of both the transmitter and the receiver. By

chance, Marconi tried putting one of the metal plates on the ground while holding the other one in the air and found he could increase his transmitting distance to one kilometer, or about one-half mile. Logically, then, he assumed that bigger metal plates placed farther apart might be even more effective. Since there was a limit to the size of the plates he could hold in the air, Marconi toyed with other methods and soon replaced the aerial metal plate with copper wires that could be lifted high overhead. This was the first radio antenna.

Constantly searching for ways to push the limits of his wireless unit, Marconi sent his brother out on walks armed with a receiver, a hat, and a pole. If he was receiving the signal that Guglielmo was sending, he responded by waving the hat on the pole. The next question was, Did these waves travel only in straight lines or could they climb the slope of a hill and go down the other side? To answer this, Marconi packed off his brother again, this time armed with a shotgun instead of a pole and a hat. After his brother had disappeared over a hill, Guglielmo sent out his signal and listened for the gunshot that would tell him he had chalked up another success. As Marconi had hoped, the waves had no trouble getting over the hill to the receiver.

As Marconi was perfecting his invention, he was rewarded for a past act of kindness. He used to read to a neighbor who was growing blind, and in gratitude

Marconi sends the first wireless message from a ship at sea to the United States.

the neighbor had taught him Morse code. While his waves were being sent several miles over hills, Marconi remembered his neighbor's lessons and began to wonder if his transmitter could be used to relay messages in Morse code.

By this time, 1895, Marconi had finally convinced his father that he had something worth pursuing, but he could not convince the Italian government to offer any assistance. So when he was 21 years old, Marconi moved to his mother's native country, Great Britain, where there was a great deal of interest in wireless telegraphy. There he got off to a terrible start when his valuable equipment was broken by suspicious customs officials, but he was eventually granted a patent and provided with the backing to make his idea a success.

By 1896, Marconi was able to send a message in Morse code over nine miles, an accomplishment that gained him worldwide fame. The following year, a nearly unsuccessful attempt to transmit over water was saved when Marconi increased the length of the antenna from 30 to 50 yards. He again proved his wireless telegraph was workable in 1898 when he sent over 100 messages from the royal yacht, 18 miles at sea, to Queen Victoria in England.

From that point to the present, it has only been a matter of farther, bigger, and better. In 1899, Marconi successfully beamed messages across the English Channel. A ship-to-shore communications system was installed at the dangerous

Strait of Dover off the coast of England and was immediately credited with saving many lives as well as priceless cargo. In 1902, Marconi showed that, by using balloons and kites to boost reception, radio waves could follow the curve of the earth and could even span the Atlantic Ocean. Less than a decade after Marconi officially invented the wireless telegraph, it was widely used in providing directions for lost ships, aiding rescue missions, giving warnings of weather conditions, and providing news service to previously inaccessible places.

Modern Communication

As with any great invention, others quickly carried the idea far beyond what the inventor had ever dreamed. Before long, the dots and dashes of Morse code were replaced with actual voices and music. Transmitting systems were able to change sounds into electric signals and transport them over hundreds of miles until they were picked up by a receiver, which converted the waves back into sounds. With further research, it was discovered that black-and-white images—and later, color

This tangle of wires was Minnesota's first radio station, pictured in 1914.

24

Three broadcasters cover a 1931 golf tournament from a mobile radio unit (above). Their program was received by radios that probably looked something like this one from the 1930s (below).

images as well—could be sent in the same way, which created television, and that waves could be bounced off an orbiting satellite to give unlimited range over the earth.

Today the earth's vast communication empire beams thousands of waves into the air every second. With such a bombardment of news, weather, music, sports, and other information and entertainment, we seldom stop to think about how it gets from the transmitter to the little boxes in our homes. For most people, getting along without these waves is almost unthinkable, but easy communication is all a fairly recent and unexpected gift from Guglielmo Marconi.

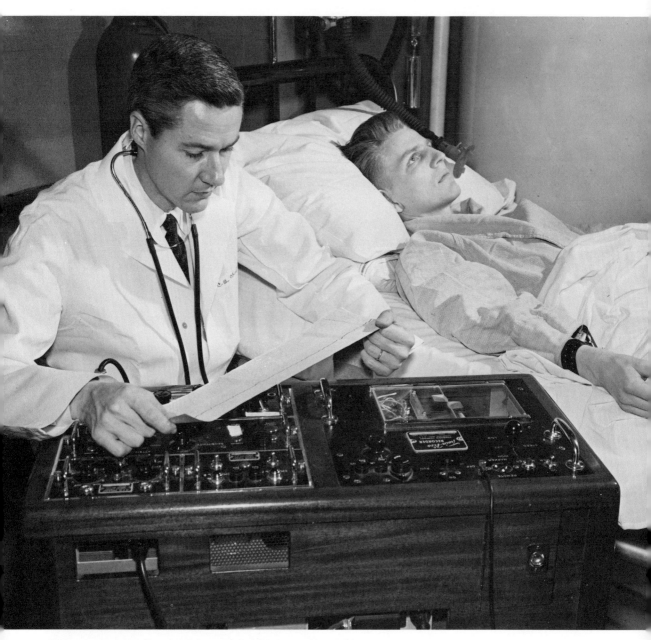

This electrocardiograph was used in the early 1950s.

3

The Electrocardiograph: Messages From the Heart

If you gain nothing else from watching television shows about hospitals, you will probably at least learn that doctors frequently order something called an EKG when dealing with very sick patients. An EKG, or electrocardiograph, may sound like a highly complicated medical instrument, but it is actually a fairly simple tool that has been routinely used to diagnose heart problems for more than 60 years. In spite of the new discoveries that are constantly being made in the medical field, the EKG is no less important today than it was in 1924 when Willem Einthoven won a Nobel Prize for physiology or medicine for its development.

The heart is one of the most important human organs, and when it starts to break down, the body is in grave danger. This organ is responsible for pumping blood containing essential supplies such as food and oxygen to all the cells of the body, which need a complete change of blood every minute. The average person needs to squeeze about three billion beats out of his or her heart by age 70 and can't afford to miss many of them. Doctors know that if there's something seriously wrong with a patient, the heart is one of the most likely sources of trouble. In the United States, heart malfunction is not only the number one killer, but it also causes more deaths than all other injuries or diseases *put together*. Yet until the development of the EKG, the heart was an extremely difficult organ to examine.

Electricity in the Body

The secret of gaining access to the condition of the heart began slowly unraveling 200 years ago when it was shown that the body conducts electric current. This was proven thanks to four good sports who held hands while one was subjected to a painful shock. The shock traveled from person to person, jolting not just one but all four members of the chain. Experiments with frogs in the 1790s then showed that electricity can do more than just travel through a body; when it is applied to a muscle, it causes that muscle to move.

In the middle of the 19th century, a pair of German scientists, Rudolph von Kölliker and Heinrich Muller, removed a nerve and the muscle it was connected to from a test animal and placed the cut end of the nerve on a beating heart. Every time the heart beat, the muscle contracted. The resulting suspicion that there must be an electric current in the heart was proven in 1878 with **electrodes**, small pieces of metal that conduct electricity, attached directly to the hearts of test animals. Logically, it could then be assumed that there is electric current in the human heart as well, but no one was about to open somebody up just to test

Augustus Waller was the first to detect electricity in the human heart.

Willem Einthoven

this theory. A man named Augustus Waller made such drastic measures unnecessary when, in 1887, he was able to detect the presence of electricity in a human heart with electrodes placed on the surface of the body.

Gradually doctors began to get a picture of the human body as a complex electrical system run by the brain. Every movement, from the twitching of an eyelid to the pounding of a fist; every thought, from deciding what to eat for dinner to figuring out complicated equations; and every

feeling, from joy to anger, is produced by an electric current.

The heart, being a muscle, is of course included in this network. Every time it contracts, doctors reasoned, there must be an electric current that accompanies the contraction. It follows, then, that any disease or injury that disrupts the heart's electrical activity can affect this important organ. For example, since nerves are the conductors of current in the body, an injured nerve can alter or even stop an electrical impulse and cause damage to the heart. Doctors theorized that if they could detect abnormal electrical activity going on in the heart, they might be able to pinpoint the problem and correct it. The problem was how to detect and display these abnormalities in a readable fashion, and this is where Willem Einthoven became involved.

The EKG

Willem Einthoven was born in the Dutch East Indies in 1860. When Willem was 10, his father—a physician—died, and the family moved to the Netherlands. Einthoven followed his father into the medical profession, but he also kept alive an interest in physics and a wide range of other scientific fields. It was while teaching at the University of Leiden that Einthoven applied his knowledge of physics and medicine to the task of measuring electricity in the heart.

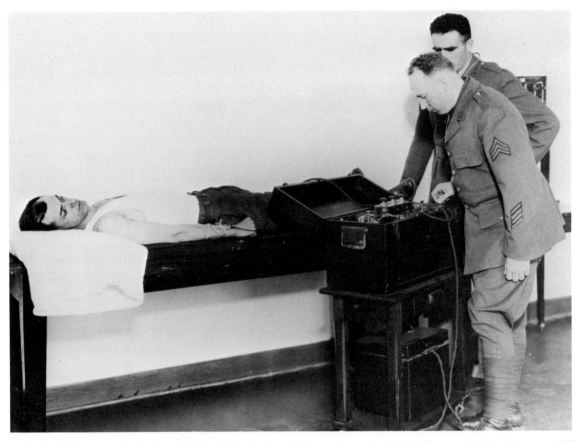

By the 1930s, the electrocardiograph had shrunk from its original 800 pounds, but it was still a large, heavy piece of equipment.

Previously, some doctors had tried to measure the heart's electrical activity with a device called a capillary electrometer, a very crude instrument that used a tiny tube of mercury to measure electricity. But this thermometerlike tool was not very precise. In 1903, Einthoven tried a different approach using what he called a string galvanometer. This consisted of

a delicate wire placed between the two arms, or poles, of a horseshoe magnet. When an electric current passed through the wire, the magnet pulled the wire away from its center position. The stronger the current, the more the wire was drawn toward one pole of the magnet. Einthoven's string galvanometer was sensitive enough to detect the subtle changes in electric current that take place in the body.

Einthoven gradually improved his machine until he had developed the electrocardiograph, an instrument that can detect electrical activity in the heart when attached to the outside of a person's body by wires and electrodes. He also tried to determine what different patterns of current indicate about the condition of the heart. Einthoven's original machine weighed over 800 pounds and took up so much room that it couldn't be moved from his laboratory to the hospital. The only way the hospital could use it was to run more than 1,500 meters (about a mile) of wire from the patient to the machine.

Although the unit has been streamlined, the materials used to make it have been improved, and adjustments have been made in recording methods, the modern EKG is remarkably similar to the machine Einthoven developed over half a century ago. The process causes no discomfort

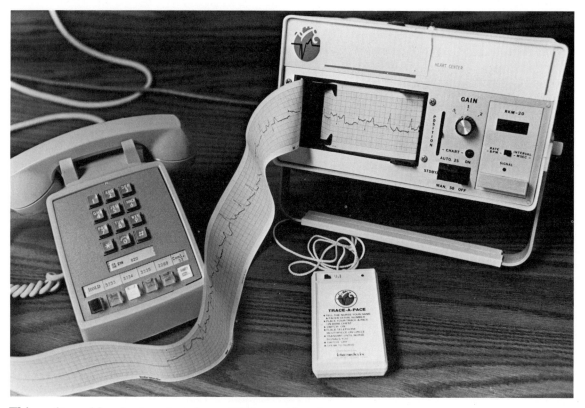

This unit enables doctors to take an EKG over the phone.

to the patient. Electrodes coated with a sodium substance that helps to conduct electricity are placed on the patient's chest where they can pick up the weak currents produced by the heart. The electrodes carry the electricity to a threadlike piece of platinum or quartz that is coated with silver to aid conduction. This thread, which may have a diameter of as little as .002 millimeters (about .00008 of an inch), hangs between the two poles of a horseshoe magnet. The electric currents from the heart cause the thread to move back and forth, and these movements are recorded.

The methods of recording the results of an EKG can vary. One way involves sending a beam of light through the space between the poles of the magnet and recording the shadows produced by the string on a moving strip of photographic paper. The final result is a long, jagged line called an electrocardiogram. As Einthoven realized, however, the results of an EKG don't mean anything unless they can be interpreted properly. A large library of "normal" readings had to be built up before doctors could recognize readings that indicated a problem.

Diagnosing Heart Problems

Today an experienced physician can use an EKG not only to determine whether or not there is heart damage, but also to locate where the problem is occurring. The heart has four chambers, the right and left atria and the right and left ventricles. All heartbeats are sparked by an electrical impulse from an area of the right atrium called the sinoatrial node

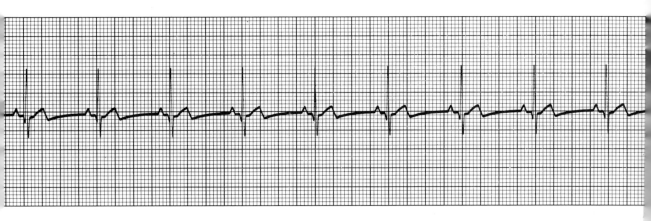

The jagged line of an electrocardiogram saves countless lives every day.

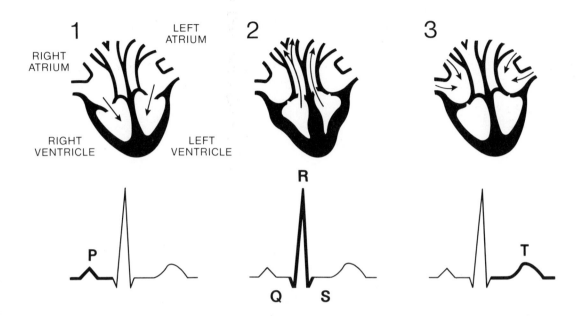

1 RIGHT ATRIUM LEFT ATRIUM RIGHT VENTRICLE LEFT VENTRICLE

2 R Q S

3 T

P

An electrocardiogram gives doctors a "picture" of the activity of the heart. The contraction of the atria, which pumps blood into the ventricles, is represented by the P wave (1). The contraction of the ventricles, which pumps blood out of the heart, is represented by the QRS wave (2). The period of rest while the atria are refilling with blood is represented by the T wave (3).

(or S-A node). The impulse makes the atria contract, and then, after a momentary delay, it causes the ventricles to contract. An EKG gives separate readings for the contraction of the atria, the contraction of the ventricles, and the period of rest before the next S-A spark.

The EKG shows abnormal electrical current in most cases of heart disease, including heart attack, heart enlargement, inflammation, and irregular rhythms. It is used in suspected cases of heart attack,

rheumatic fever, and drug overdose, and it enables doctors to diagnose the causes of such symptoms as chest pain, fainting, abnormal heartbeat, and shortness of breath. The procedure is so quick and easy that it allows doctors to pinpoint a problem before it gets worse and begin treatment immediately. Although Einthoven was awarded the Nobel Prize for his invention back in 1924, the electrocardiograph still saves countless numbers of lives every day.

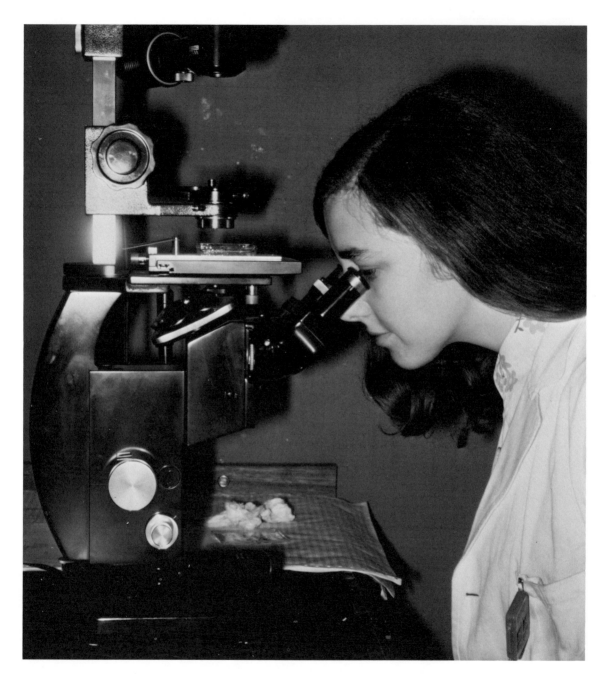

4

The Phase Contrast Microscope: The Invisible Made Visible

Science researchers are often accused of subscribing to the twisted notion that the only way to study living things is to kill them. When you think of all the learning that is done by cutting up frogs, mice, and cats and by examining jars of pickled larvae and mountings of dead insects, that sometimes seems to be the case. This doesn't necessarily happen by choice, however. A scientist would rather study a live animal than a dead one whenever possible; after all, a dead organism may reveal something about anatomy, but only a live organism can show a scientist how it works.

The phase contrast microscope enabled scientists to view transparent organisms without staining them first with poisonous dye.

For many years, microbiologists searched for ways to study cells and microorganisms without killing them. Unfortunately, many of these microscopic bundles of life are transparent, which makes them almost invisible under a normal microscope. They could be made to show up—sometimes with great clarity—if a dye were added to them, but dyes were basically poisons. So until a better way was found to make the invisible visible, scientists were faced with a choice of looking at a dead bit of matter or not seeing anything at all.

What Does *Invisible* Mean?

In order to find a way to make transparent objects visible, scientists first had to understand why they were invisible.

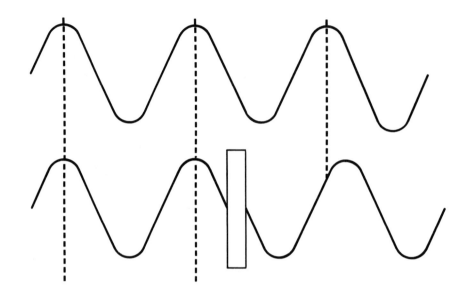

These two light waves start out in phase with each other, which means that they both reach their highest and lowest points at the same time and the tops of the waves line up. But when the second wave passes through a transparent object, the wave is slowed so that the tops of the waves no longer line up. This is called a phase change.

The difference between an opaque, or nontransparent, object and a transparent object is the amount of light they absorb. When light waves hit an opaque object, some of the waves are absorbed, reducing the **intensity**, or brightness, of the light the object lets through. The more light an object absorbs, the darker it appears to be. The human eye is able to detect the changes in the brightness of the light and, therefore, can see an opaque object. A completely transparent object, on the other hand, does not absorb light. Because there is no change in the intensity of the light passing through the object, there is nothing for the eye to see.

Just because transparent objects don't absorb light doesn't mean they let the waves pass through completely unaltered. When a light wave passes through a transparent object, it is slowed down slightly and reaches the eye a fraction of a second later than it would have if the object hadn't been there. This is called a **phase change**, which means that the times that the light wave reaches its highest and lowest points have changed (see diagram above).

If the eye could detect phase changes, then transparent objects would be visible. But the eye can't see a phase change unless the change is large enough to cause a difference in the intensity of the light. This happens when a light wave is slowed down to the point that its phase is the opposite of the phase of a nearby light wave that hasn't been slowed. In other words, when the slowed wave is at its lowest point, the other wave is at its highest (see diagram below). This causes the two light waves to **interfere**, or collide, until they've cancelled each other out. The result is a dark area that the eye can see. Unfortunately for microbiologists, a transparent object doesn't cause enough of a phase change to be visible. Until the development of Frits Zernike's phase contrast microscope, these objects remained invisible.

Zernike and the Ghost Image

Born in 1888 in Amsterdam, the Netherlands, Frits Zernike combined his skill at working with machines with an impressive background in the formal academic world. As a child, he was as at ease winning

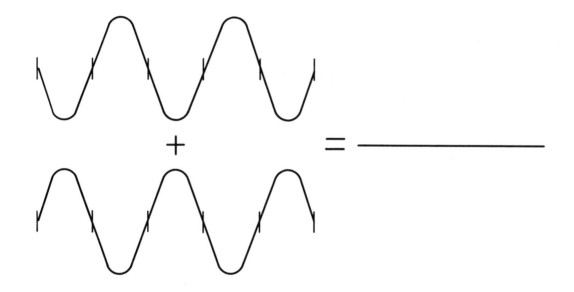

These two light waves are in opposite phases, which means that one reaches its highest point at the same time the other reaches its lowest point. This causes the two waves to collide, or interfere, and cancel each other out, leaving a straight line that the eye sees as a dark area.

Frits Zernike

mathematics contests as he was building an observatory from scratch. By the time he was 27, Zernike had become a leader in the fields of chemistry and physics.

During his scientific career, which was spent entirely at the University of Groningen in the Netherlands, Zernike tackled optical problems of great complexity. In the course of his studies, he discovered a fascinating bit of information about light waves. Zernike noticed that certain mirrors that were not perfectly constructed reflected a double image of an object, as if there were ghost lines just slightly off the real image. He explained that the ghost image was created by an irregularity in the mirror that caused some of the reflected light to be half a wavelength out of phase with the rest of the light. With a little work, Zernike found that he could get rid of the ghost image. He made phase strips, glass plates with etched grooves in them, which brought the light from the two images into the same phase so that only one image was reflected.

At this point, Zernike's observations seemed to be of little importance except as a way to correct irregularities in the surfaces of mirrors. But a key characteristic of inventors is that they are able to take a set of facts and apply them in areas where few people would think of using them. Zernike knew that, like phase strips, transparent objects alter the phase of the light that passes through them. He wondered if he could use a phase strip to increase the change in the phase of the light passing through a transparent object enough to cause a change in intensity that the eye could see. If used with a microscope, this would make transparent microorganisms visible.

The Secret Microscope

Zernike based his invention on a standard microscope. To this he added a

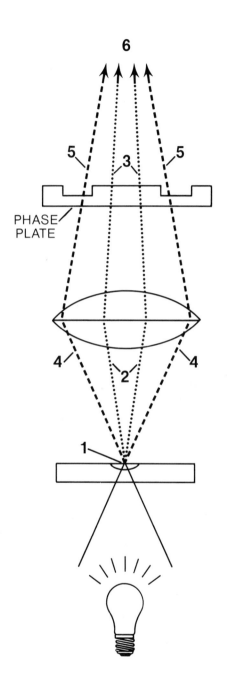

PHASE
PLATE

device that concentrated light into a narrow cone and a phase strip. He replaced the etched lines on the phase strip, or phase plate as it is called today, with a ring-shaped groove in the glass.

The process of changing the phase of the light waves was really fairly simple (see diagram, left). The cone of light was focused on the transparent specimen that was to be viewed (1). Some of the light passed through the specimen, undergoing a phase change (2), and was then sent through a phase plate. This light was channeled away from the groove and through the thicker part of the glass to make it undergo another phase change (3). Meanwhile, the light that went around the specimen (4) was channeled through the groove in the phase plate (5). Because the groove made the glass thinner at that point, there was almost no change at all in the phase of this light.

When the two kinds of light were brought back together after passing through the phase plate (6), they were very different from each other. The light that had passed through the specimen and the thick part of the phase plate had undergone two phase changes and was now in the opposite phase of the light that had gone around. The waves interfered with each other enough to make the transparent specimen visible.

Excited about his new invention, which he called a phase contrast microscope, Zernike brought it to an influential laboratory in Jena, Germany, in the mid-1930s.

The reaction there was indifference; Zernike was told that if his microscope was of any real use, the Jena lab would have invented it long ago. Shortly thereafter, Zernike's phase contrast microscope was forgotten in the chaos of World War II. It wasn't until United States soldiers occupying Jena in 1945 stumbled across two of Zernike's microscopes that the secret was out. Curious as to the nature of these tools, the Americans sent them back to the United States for examination. Almost immediately, news of their value spread, and phase contrast microscopes were in demand all over the world.

The phase contrast microscope opened up a whole new area for study. Microorganisms could be viewed without the use of poisonous dyes. Scientists were able to zero in on minute living cells to observe the functions of such cell structures as the mitochondria, to study all the changes that occur when living cells divide, and to inspect differences in tissues that previously had seemed identical. Geneticists could get a look at the obscure chromosomes, the intracellular structures containing the genes that dictate what

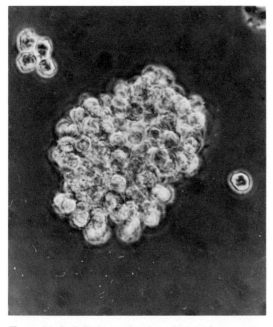 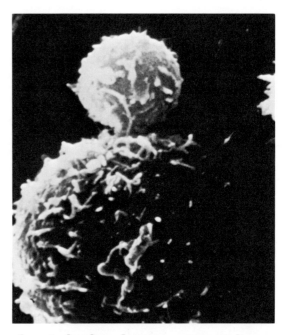

Even Nobel Prize-winning inventions are replaced as technology becomes more and more advanced, as is shown by these two photographs of cells in different stages of genetic engineering. While the phase contrast image (left) shows details of cells without the use of dyes, the electron microscope photograph (right) gives an even closer view of similar cells.

40

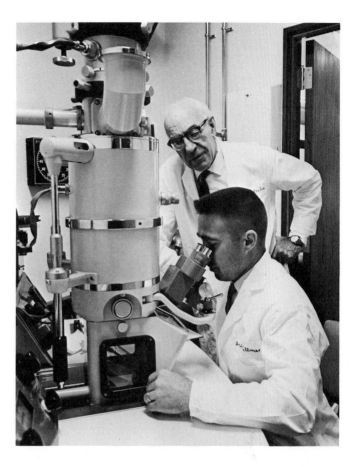

The phase contrast microscope was an important step on the way to the development of the electron microscope, pictured here.

characteristics will be passed on to the next generation. The phase contrast microscope proved especially useful in giving a close-up view of the live runaway killer cells that cause cancer. Zernike's invention also found practical use in the industrial world as it gave research and development teams a better view of the makeup of such tiny transparent objects as crystals, oils, soaps, clay, dust, food, plastics, and textiles.

The phase contrast microscope did not prove to be the ultimate tool to probe the "invisible" world—in fact, techniques using the electron microscope and laser technology can delve much deeper into that area. But for creating a breakthrough into ways to explore microbiology and in paving the way for future microscopic development, Frits Zernike was awarded a well-deserved Nobel Prize for physics in 1953.

5

The Transistor:
Enter the Computer Age

For a quick example of how the inventing process has changed in the past century, consider this question: Who invented the incandescent light bulb? You probably know that it was Thomas Alva Edison, and you may even know where and when it happened and how the invention works. Now answer this question: Who invented the computer? Although the computer is just as important as the light bulb, chances are you have no idea who was responsible for it.

As we near the 21st century, it is becoming more and more difficult to identify the creator of a new invention or even to understand what that invention does. The computer was the result of a seemingly endless series of modifications involving many corporations and a long list of people. Computers have brought such enormous benefit to society that it seems that someone involved in their creation should have been awarded the Nobel Prize. This did, in fact, happen in 1956 when the Nobel Prize for physics was awarded for the invention of the device that made the modern computer possible—the transistor. But even at that early stage, the Nobel committee found it impossible to honor a single hero, and the award went to a research team made up of three scientists: William Shockley, Walter Brattain, and John Bardeen.

Not one of the three men was thinking specifically about computers as he worked at Bell Laboratories, the research division

Computers have become an important tool in most businesses.

Many important inventions, including the transistor, have come out of the Bell Laboratories (pictured here in 1949).

of American Telephone and Telegraph. Bell had hired the three highly trained scientists to explore the behavior of **electrons**—tiny negatively charged particles—in solids in the hope that one of them might make a discovery that could be used to improve the company's communications systems.

By the 1930s, telephone systems were becoming too complex for the cumbersome mechanical switches that operated them, and Bell Laboratories wanted to replace the mechanical switch with an efficient electronic switch. They needed a switch that could **rectify** current, which means it would allow the current

to travel in only one direction at a time. The switch also had to be able to turn the current on and off. There was a device called a **vacuum tube** that could perform both of these functions as well as **amplifying**—or increasing the strength of—the signal sent by the current, but Bell was hoping to discover something even more advanced than the vacuum tube.

Semiconductors

When Walter Brattain and William Shockley began working together at Bell in the late 1930s, they were especially interested in a kind of solid known as a **semiconductor**. A semiconductor is a material that conducts electricity better than an insulator, which blocks current, but not as well as a metal, which allows electricity to flow freely. The men's attention was captured by the fact that semiconductors such as the mineral galena had been used to rectify electronic signals in early crystal radio sets. The two were excited by the possibility that semiconductors could somehow be the key ingredient in the switch that Bell was looking for and, if the material could be made to amplify signals, might even replace the vacuum tube. Brattain and Shockley tried to develop an amplifying switch using the semiconductor copper oxide, but their work was interrupted by World War II.

This telephone switchboard is a replica of one used in 1878. Outdated mechanical switches were still used in telephone systems as late as the 1930s.

John Bardeen (left), William Shock-ley (center), and Walter Brattain (right) meet in 1972 to mark the 25th anniversary of their Nobel Prize-winning invention.

After the war, Brattain and Shockley, who had both been doing defense research, returned to the study of semiconductors and were joined by physicist John Bardeen. The three scientists knew that in order to conduct electricity, a material must have some free electrons to "pick up" a current and carry it from one side of the material to the other. Team leader Shockley proposed that if a semiconductor was exposed to a certain kind of current (either positive or negative, depending on the semiconductor), the current would add more free electrons to the material and increase its conductivity—or turn the electricity on. Similarly, another kind of current (again, either positive or negative) would trap the free electrons and decrease the conductivity—or turn the electricity off.

The research team was sure that Shockley had found the switch they were looking for, but when they put it to the test, they were surprised to find it didn't function. Bardeen and Brattain immediately went to work to find out why. It was Bardeen who suggested that the current was only affecting the electrons on the surface of the semiconductor because it couldn't pierce the surface barrier to get to the electrons on the inside. Bardeen and Brattain found that if they placed two pieces of wire, called contacts, very close together on the surface of the semiconductor and sent a positive current through one of the contacts, the current would poke a hole in the surface barrier and pass through to a base made of metal on the other side. They finally had their switch.

Bardeen and Brattain were in for another surprise. While toying with their switch, trying to speed up the response time,

they discovered something unusual was happening. When the current passed between one contact and the base, a much larger version of the signal was passed between the other contact and the base. Small changes in the current in the first contact point could greatly change the power output at the other. The scientists called this transfer of resistance, and the device was named a transfer resistor, or transistor for short.

This first transistor—the point contact transistor—was replaced within a month by Shockley's junction transistor, the forerunner of what is commonly referred

The point contact transistor (left) was invented by the Bell research team in 1947. This primitive-looking apparatus was soon replaced by the junction transistor (right).

47

Lee De Forest, who was fascinated by wireless telegraphy, invented the vacuum tube to amplify radio signals.

to turn electricity on and off in as little as 1/1,000 of a microsecond (a microsecond is 1/1,000,000 of a second) to develop a card translator, a device that could rapidly route long-distance phone calls through their network. The transistor's amplifying function was put to use in hearing aids. A weak electronic signal directed to the transistor could come out 100,000 times more powerful than it went in!

Shrinking the Computer

So far, we haven't made any connection between the work of Shockley, Bardeen, and Brattain and the world of computers. Until the development of the transistor, the flow of electricity in computers, as well as in other electronic equipment, was controlled by the vacuum tube. The startling efficiency of the transistor in starting, stopping, rectifying, and amplifying electric current—everything a vacuum tube could do—could not have been discovered at a better time. There were problems with the vacuum tube that had brought computer technology to a standstill—problems that could be solved by the transistor.

The most obvious difference between a vacuum tube and a transistor was size. Although not much larger than your thumb, vacuum tubes were far too bulky for computers. When one small vacuum tube was multiplied by the thousands of

to as the computer chip. This device was constructed like a three-layer sandwich in which the two contact points are on the outer layers with the base in the middle.

After three years of intensive fine tuning, the Bell research team demonstrated their findings in June 1948. Despite the bewildering terminology and the abstract theory behind it, Bell officials were quick to see the practical possibilities in the transistor. They used its ability

tubes needed to operate even a modest computer and then added to the miles of wiring it took to connect all the tubes to the power source, the equipment filled a fair-sized room. In contrast, the first transistors were so small that 50 of them could fit into the space occupied by just one vacuum tube, and further miniaturization has produced transistors that can only be seen with a microscope. The tiny transistor has made it possible for computers to shrink to the size of a typewriter and even smaller.

Size was not the only trouble with vacuum tubes; they were also very expensive to operate. All those tubes took a great deal of power and ran the risk of overheating. Vacuum tubes were unreliable and often failed without warning, having to be replaced; and even if they performed as they should, the tubes did not have a long life. By the time the transistor was invented, the most powerful computers had almost reached the point at which maintenance people would have had to spend 24 hours a day just replacing defective tubes!

The transistor, however, is so inexpensive that transistor-operated machines have come to be considered almost disposable items. The cost of pocket calculators, for example, decreased more than a hundredfold in 10 years at a time when inflation was driving up the price

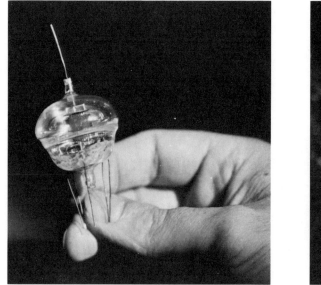

The vacuum tube (left) looks bulky and old fashioned next to the two silicon wafers sitting on the eye of a needle (right). The wafers contain several tiny transistors.

of everything else. The efficient transistor uses about 1/1,000,000 the power of a vacuum tube while giving off no heat at all. The initial cost of transistors is low because they are made out of the inexpensive semiconductor silicon, and they don't have to be replaced because they never wear out.

One of the main reasons for using a computer is that it can perform certain functions much faster than the human brain. Although the electrical impulses that travel through vacuum tubes move at the speed of light, in early computers, the many miles of wire the current had to cover caused delays in obtaining information. Once the tubes were replaced by transistors, the distance that the electricity had to travel through the "switches" was reduced to microscopic

The computer has become a common feature in many school classrooms.

size, and the response time was slashed to unimaginably short units of time. Even the delay from the warm-up time the tubes needed in order to function properly was eliminated.

Saving Millions of Years

Production of transistors has become a billion-dollar-a-year business in the United States, and the changes these tiny devices have caused in our world are staggering. Nearly every area of life has been touched by this one invention, which has, in a short time, spawned countless other inventions. Because a computer can do things that would take a human millions of years to do, it enables scientists and inventors to easily solve problems that would have been unsolvable 20 years ago. With their almost unlimited capacity for storing and processing data, computers can, in an instant, produce information from all over the world on a screen—information that would have taken a lifetime for a human to dig up.

Name any activity and there are sure to be computers involved: from banking to controlling air traffic, from football scouting to farming to budgeting family finances. The entire space program could not have gotten off the ground, much less to the moon, without lightning-fast figuring from computers. They have revolutionized business by streamlining information files, organizing accounting methods, handling payrolls, analyzing marketing information, replacing typing with word processing, and predicting future events. Our educational system now leans heavily on computers as an aid in learning, even at the preschool level. Lifesaving medical techniques such as the CT scan came about only because of computers.

Add to all that the various uses of transistors in such equipment as televisions, radios, telephones, radar, automobile ignitions, cameras, and so on, and you can see the enormous effect that the unexpected discovery by Shockley, Bardeen, and Brattain has had on the world. In fact, the only way you could calculate the impact would be with an enormously powerful computer!

Radiocarbon dating of Olmec ruins like this one in La Venta Park in Mexico have enabled archaeologists to place the beginnings of the Olmec civilization in the 13th century B.C.

6

Radiocarbon Dating: Uncovering the Mysteries of the Past

Is there anything so fascinating and, at the same time, so maddening as a mystery? Questions without answers, brainteasers without solutions, and facts without explanations challenge our minds and torture our curiosities. We stand in awe of the Sherlock Holmes type of detective who can read clues that say nothing to the average person. Perhaps the greatest mysteries of all involve the earth's distant past because the witnesses are all gone, the evidence has been scattered, and the answers seem to be buried forever. And perhaps the greatest detectives of all are the archaeologists who piece together stories from trails that have been cold for centuries.

A strong case could be made that the greatest tracker-detective of all time was a professor named Willard F. Libby. Using the radiocarbon dating methods that Libby pioneered, archaeologists and anthropologists are able to gauge the age of a material and thereby reconstruct the order of events of thousands of years ago, even those that occurred long before humans appeared on earth.

Radioactivity Everywhere

Willard F. Libby was born in Grand Valley, Colorado, in 1908. He started his academic career in the humble setting of a two-room country schoolhouse and by the age of 25 had earned a Ph.D. Libby became interested in nuclear physics while working for the United States government in its massive effort to crack the secrets of atomic energy during World War II. After the war, he joined the faculty of the University of Chicago's Institute of Nuclear Studies.

One of the elements Libby worked with was carbon; more specifically, he was interested in that tiny percentage of

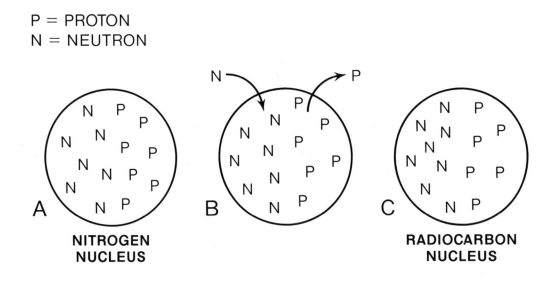

P = PROTON
N = NEUTRON

A
**NITROGEN
NUCLEUS**

B

C
**RADIOCARBON
NUCLEUS**

carbon **atoms** that are **radioactive**. (A radioactive atom is one whose nucleus, or core, is breaking apart and giving off energy.) How do these few carbon atoms become radioactive? Libby's work showed that it all starts with **cosmic rays**–tiny high-energy particles that are constantly bombarding the gases of the earth's upper atmosphere. When cosmic rays strike an atom, the **protons** and **neutrons** that make up its **nucleus** are released into the atmosphere. Libby theorized that the released free neutrons are absorbed by nitrogen atoms, but he knew that an atom can't take on another neutron without undergoing a change itself.

Nitrogen (see diagram) has a **mass number** of 14, which means its nucleus ordinarily contains 14 particles: 7 protons and 7 neutrons (A). But when a nitrogen atom absorbs a free neutron, its whole system is knocked out of order. To keep its mass number of 14, the nitrogen atom has to kick out a proton (B), leaving it with 6 protons and 8 neutrons (C). An element is identified by the number of protons in its nuclei. For instance, if a nucleus contains 7 protons, it is part of a nitrogen atom, and if a nucleus contains 6 protons, it belongs to a carbon atom. So, by replacing a proton with a neutron, the nitrogen atom changes into a carbon atom with a mass number of 14 instead of carbon's usual 12. This element is a radioactive form of carbon known as carbon 14, or radiocarbon.

Libby realized that if radiocarbon is constantly being produced, then a small amount of this radioactive element must be present in gases that contain carbon, including carbon dioxide. Because plants take in carbon dioxide, and all animals feed on plants or on plant-eaters, Libby concluded that every living thing contains radiocarbon and must therefore be slightly radioactive. Libby's observations might seem to be nothing but interesting bits of trivia, but he uncovered some facts about radiocarbon that showed his findings to be much more important than they first appeared to be.

Libby found that the radioactive composition of a living thing is in a state of equilibrium—as long as the organism is alive, it takes in new radiocarbon at the same rate at which it loses it. At the instant of death, however, the organism stops taking in radiocarbon and only releases it as the radiocarbon decays.

No matter how much of the radioactive element there is and no matter where it is located, radiocarbon always has a **half-life** of about 5,730 years. This means that from the moment a sample starts to decay, it takes 5,730 years for half of its radiocarbon to disintegrate. In another 5,730 years, the half that is left will have disintegrated by half, leaving a fourth of the original, and so on. For example, if a tree containing 16 units of radiocarbon is chopped down, in 5,730

years the radiocarbon will decrease by half to 8 units. In another 5,730 years, the radiocarbon will again disintegrate by half to 4 units, and so on. Every time the amount of radiocarbon decreases by half, the speed at which it decays must also decrease by half. In the example, the tree lost 8 units of radiocarbon the first 5,730 years, but only 4 units the second. Libby was able to put all of this information together to develop radiocarbon dating.

History and Half-lives

The underlying principle of radiocarbon dating is not difficult. To determine the age of a sample, scientists measure the rate at which its radiocarbon is decaying and compare it to the known rate of decay of organisms that have just died. For instance, if a sample is found to be losing atoms at half the rate at which a recently dead sample is losing them, it must be approximately 5,730 years old. Libby was not the first to point out the connection between radioactivity and the age of a material. Back in 1905, Lord Ernest Rutherford had suggested that radioactive properties could be used to measure geological time. But Libby was the man who, working largely alone and unnoticed, was able to combine all the facts into a system and show that it could work.

Those most concerned with times gone by, such as anthropologists, geologists, and archaeologists, joined with Libby in testing the laboratory methods for radiocarbon dating, and by the late 1940s, a procedure had been refined. A sample was chopped finely and purified to get the 10 grams of carbon needed for the test. The carbon, which was part radiocarbon and part regular carbon, was then burned to produce carbon dioxide gas, which was funneled into an instrument called a geiger counter. The geiger counter measured the rate at which the radiocarbon was decaying, and this number was used to determine the age of the sample.

Libby's dating method was soon ready to be tested using some ancient materials whose ages were already known. Although it must have pained archaeologists to allow it, Libby chopped up a sample of the funeral boat of King Sesotris III of Egypt and put it to the radiocarbon test. His results showed the boat to be 3,621 years old, just off the known age of 3,750. Libby also tested ashes from a Roman camp and a piece of cloth from the Dead Sea Scrolls. In each case, the carbon-dating method produced results within 5 to 10 percent of the actual age.

Although some archaeologists scoffed at radiocarbon dating as a very crude measuring instrument, other scholars declared that it was the greatest tool for dating material that had ever been produced. People had suspected that the earth was much older than anyone had dreamed ever since excavations during

Willard F. Libby

the 19th century had revealed that some areas in England had at various times been above the water and at other times under the sea, but they had no proof. With the new method of radiocarbon dating, scientists could at last get a feel for the ages of the earth and its artifacts.

It is easy to think that the usefulness of radiocarbon dating is limited to bones, teeth, and ashes since the method only works with once-living samples. But the category of things that were once alive also includes cloth, plankton, seabeds, peat bogs, sediment, limestone, and objects made of wood. When Libby first

56

developed radiocarbon dating, he could fairly accurately date items that were up to 30,000 years old. Since then, improvements have been made that allow reasonably accurate dating to about 65,000 years and require much smaller samples than Libby used. Geologists have built on Libby's discoveries by using readings of other radioactive materials with tremendously long half-lives to date rocks and minerals. Using uranium or potassium elements with half-lives of millions of years, scholars can get an even more accurate idea of how old a world we are living in.

Surprising Findings

Thanks to the revolutionary process of radiocarbon dating, scientists have uncovered surprising facts about the history of the earth and its people. Both now appear to be older than anything we can imagine, the earth being untold millions of years old and our species perhaps as old as 500,000 years. With new dating methods, it is now possible to study more carefully the cycles of climate change in our world. It was once widely believed that the last ice age occurred about 25,000 years ago. Recently, however, birchwood samples from the retreating edge of an ice cap were discovered to be closer to 10,000 years old. On the practical side, Libby's invention helps scientists to study substances such as

peat and coal to see how long it takes for usable deposits of energy-producing materials to form.

Each new clue—embers from a fire in a cave that date from over 15,000 years ago, shells from an agricultural settlement in Iraq that are almost 7,000 years old, dates for the arrival of people at a remote Pacific island and for the building of a great city in Zimbabwe, calculation of the ages of dinosaur fossils—adds to our knowledge of ourselves and of our world. The worth of Libby's dating method can be summed up in the fact that in the field of archaeology, it is almost unheard of for any report not to make use of radiocarbon data. For this giant advancement, one which aided a field entirely unrelated to his own realm of physics, Willard F. Libby was awarded the Nobel Prize for chemistry in 1960.

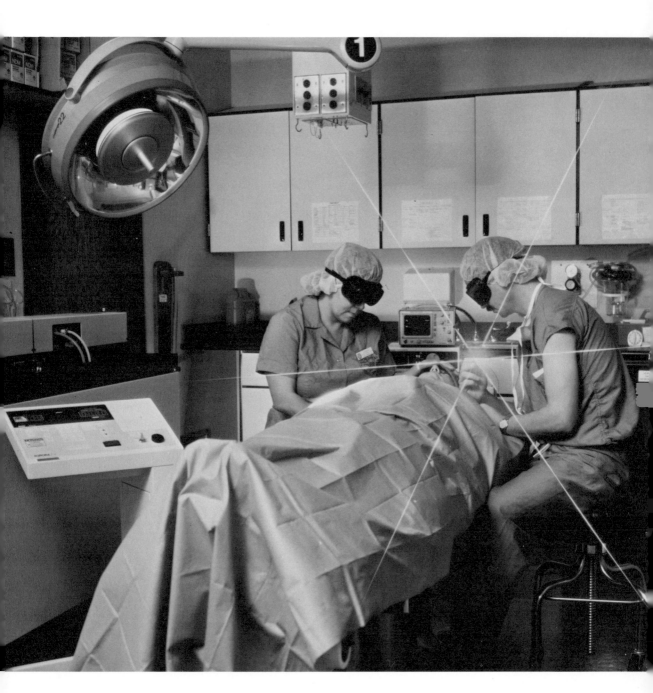

7

The Laser:
The Power of Light

If you take all the inventions ever fashioned by human hands—from the first lumpy wheel to the latest supercomputer—and add up their influences on our world, the total will still pale when compared to the importance of a single energy source whose existence owes nothing to the efforts of humankind. That energy source is the sun, the driving force behind life on earth. One of the sun's primary benefits to us is its steady supply of light, a resource with extraordinary powers that we are only just beginning to understand.

Light seems to be a pleasant, harmless

The microscopic cutting edge of a laser can be used to perform intricate eye surgery.

phenomenon and is hardly most people's idea of a mighty force. Thanks to the efforts of several talented scientists, however, we now know what lies behind that peaceful exterior. Light can be sharper than the sharpest razor and hotter than the hottest torch. It is able to bore holes into diamonds, measure distance more accurately than the best surveying equipment, patch a tiny hole better than the most delicate thread, and destroy the most powerful missile. Of course, ordinary light can't do any of these things on its own; it needs the help of an amazing instrument called the laser.

The development of the laser follows the trend of most recent inventions in that the isolated wizard in the laboratory has been replaced by a long roster of contributors. Although the first laser can

Charles Hard Townes

be traced to Dr. Theodore Maiman, who announced the successful testing of his invention on July 7, 1960, the Nobel Prize for the invention went to someone else. In the view of the Nobel selection committee, Maiman had only been following clues that had been dug out over the past half century by a number of scientists and were put together by Charles Hard Townes. Townes, a South Carolinan born in 1915, was awarded the Nobel Prize for the laser in 1964. Although he did not actually construct the first laser with his own hands, he was chosen as the scientist most responsible for its invention.

What Is Light?

Before we can understand what a laser is, we must answer the question, What is light? This was a question that baffled the best physicists for years; they couldn't decide whether light was made up of waves or separate particles. In 1900, a German named Max Planck broke some new ground in this discussion with his Nobel Prize-winning quantum theory of energy, which proposed that heat—a form of radiation—is made up of little particles, or "quanta," of energy. Five years later, the brilliant Albert Einstein took Planck's theory a step further by stating that light, which is another form of radiation, is also made up of particles. Einstein, who was awarded a Nobel Prize for his theory, called the particles of light **photons**.

These new discoveries left the scientific community even more confused about the nature of light. Light appeared to be a wave, yet respected scientists were claiming that it was made up of particles. It couldn't be both, could it? According to Einstein, this was very possible. Einstein believed that, depending on certain conditions, light could behave like both particles and waves.

In 1913, Danish physicist Niels Bohr—yet another Nobel laureate—used the information about what light is to discover where it comes from. The nucleus of an atom is surrounded by particles called electrons, which were once thought to move at random. Bohr discovered that electrons actually move in set orbits around the nucleus (see diagram, top right), and that the farther away an electron is from the nucleus, the more energy it has. He found that if certain atoms are exposed to an energy source, some of their electrons will absorb energy and jump to a higher orbit (A). But an electron can only stay at an excited state for a short time before dropping back to its original orbit and giving off the extra energy in the form of a photon—a particle of light (B). This process is called **spontaneous emission**.

Albert Einstein laid the groundwork for the concept of lasers when he theorized that there was a more controlled way, which he called **stimulated emission**, that electrons could give off photons (see diagram, bottom right). He proposed that if an electron absorbed energy in the form of a photon and jumped to a higher orbit (C) and then was hit by another photon with the same amount of energy as the first one, the electron would not absorb the second photon. Instead, while the unabsorbed photon continued on its way, the electron would emit the first photon and drop back to its original orbit. The two photons, or light particles, would be **coherent**, which means they would move away from the electron in the same direction and phase and would have identical **frequencies** and wavelengths (D). If they hit another excited electron of the same energy level, more photons would be released.

SPONTANEOUS EMISSION

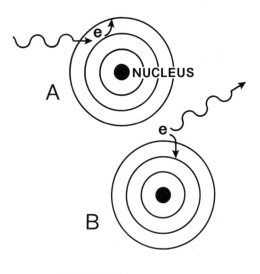

e = ELECTRON
⌇⌇⌇→ = PHOTON

STIMULATED EMISSION

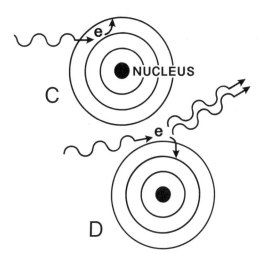

The light you see every day in ordinary sunlight and lamplight is **incoherent**—its waves have a wide variety of wavelengths and frequencies and shoot out at different phases in all directions at once. This light dissipates very rapidly because the waves collide and push each other apart. Coherent light waves, however, line up with each other, so they remain very concentrated and can be surprisingly powerful. It appeared that coherent light could be a very useful form of energy, but this was all just speculation until Charles Hard Townes set to work on the matter.

From Masers to Lasers

Charles Hard Townes was a Columbia University professor with a wide range of expertise in such diverse areas as modern languages, radar bombing systems, and electromagnetic forces. In 1954, Townes developed the maser, an instrument that takes its name from the way it works: *m*icrowave *a*mplification by *s*timulated *e*mission of *r*adiation. What this means is that the maser uses the properties of stimulated emission to cause microwaves to be coherent, or in step

This maser not only amplifies microwaves, but it can also be used as an incredibly precise clock. The machine is shown with Professor Charles Hard Townes (left), its inventor, and Dr. J. P. Gordon (right), who aided in its development.

The beam from a maser can travel long distances without dissipating. In this Bell Laboratories experiment, a phototube receives a beam flashed from a maser located 25 miles away.

with each other. This amplifies the waves, or makes them stronger. Working with his brother-in-law, Dr. Arthur Schawlow, Townes then described how his information could be used to develop a similar machine, the laser, that would concentrate light rather than microwaves.

Once Townes had broken the major developmental barriers blocking the way of the laser, a number of scientists tried to develop the machine. Dr. Theodore Maiman kept working on the project even after several leading scientists advised him to give up on it. When Maiman perfected his device in 1960, the age of

the laser had arrived—although no one was quite sure exactly what to do with the contraption.

How Does It Work?

Although it sounds intimidating, the laser (*light amplification by stimulated emission of radiation*) is basically a simple machine with only four relatively uncomplicated parts. First, there must be a lasing medium. This is a substance with electrons that can be stimulated to release photons. Maiman used a ruby as the lasing medium. Secondly, there must be an energy source to stimulate the electrons. One such energy source is a flashtube, which gives off bright flashes of light.

Once the lasing medium has absorbed all the energy it can hold, it gives off a burst of coherent light. This light is not nearly strong enough to have much use, which is the reason for the third part: a mirror-lined cavity that traps the light from the lasing medium. This cavity can be created by coating a ruby on both ends with silver so that the flashes of light keep reflecting back and forth between the two ends. Every time the light crosses the ruby, it stimulates electrons to release more photons. This produces a chain reaction of ever-increasing intensity until the light is strong enough to penetrate one of the mirrors. The fourth part of a laser is simply a device that guides this extremely powerful light toward its target.

Lasers can do amazing things. When their light is very concentrated, they produce a tremendous amount of heat. Concentrated laser light beams are millions of times brighter than ordinary sunlight, and when the brightness converts to heat, the temperatures produced can be astronomical. Laser temperatures have been recorded at more than twice that of the surface of the sun. Because laser beams are made of coherent light, they don't spread out the way a flashlight beam does. In fact, a laser beam directed to the moon held so steady that after traveling all that distance, it still illuminated an area of less than five feet! This cohesion enables the rays to retain their power over long distances and also makes them very easy to control. A laser beam can be focused to any width desired, and at extremely narrow widths, it becomes an extremely effective cutting edge.

Lasers on the Job

Lasers perform a wide array of beneficial services, and nowhere is this more evident than in the medical world. Since laser beams can be focused to a cutting edge as fine as 1/1,000,000 of an inch in diameter, they can perform microsurgery that is beyond the capability of the sharpest blade. In fact, laser beams can be made so narrow that they form "knives" sharp enough to penetrate the skin without causing bleeding or even leaving a mark! They also have the advantage of being completely germ free, so they greatly reduce the risk of infection.

Perhaps the most widely used laser adaptation in medicine is in eye surgery. Once a small hole develops in the retina of the eye, the deterioration can easily accelerate until the retina detaches and the patient loses his or her sight. But a low-power laser, carefully focused, can repair the hole by raising a tiny burn scar on it. Because the device can be focused so specifically, there is no need to worry about damaging the delicate tissues that make up the eye. In fact, lasers have been known to raise small blisters on a cell's surface without harming the rest of the cell.

The benefits of the laser are not restricted to medicine; the instrument can put on a hard hat as well. In the hands of industrial workers, the laser sheds its role as a knife and becomes an incredibly powerful and precise drill. Before the development of lasers, drilling a hole in a diamond was extremely expensive and could take as long as three days. A laser, however, can bore through even this hard material in just a few minutes without the cost of broken drill bits. And, in spite of its strength, a laser beam puts so little stress on the areas surrounding its target that laser heat can be used to drill holes in materials prone to splitting under pressure. Lasers are also used for drilling when extreme accuracy is crucial. The precision of laser heat makes it possible to etch microcircuits on computer chips so small that they can barely be seen by the human eye.

One of the more frustrating realities of machinery is that parts that need to be sealed inside a protective housing are often difficult, if not impossible, to repair when they break down. Lasers, however, can penetrate sealed tubes or shells without harming them and perform welding and soldering operations on otherwise inaccessible wires or metal parts. Laser heat is also used to flashmelt metal coatings onto other materials, allowing

This apparatus uses a laser beam to weld tiny metal parts together (above). The laser welder at work (below).

A laser technician makes adjustments on the Nova laser, one of the most powerful lasers in the world.

the creation of stronger and more durable materials.

There seems to be almost no end to the fields in which lasers have made an impact. They can be used to track flying objects, identify pollutants in the air, warn of earthquakes, moniter violations of nuclear weapons test ban treaties, and break new ground in photography. Their unwavering precision is used to line up tunnels, bridges, and high-rise buildings and has been used to measure the distance from the earth to the moon right down to the centimeter. Scanners using lasers have replaced the cash registers at the supermarket, and laser beams capable of carrying 10 million phone calls or 8,000 television programs at the same time may soon make our current systems of communication obsolete.

Unlimited Possibilities

Given the many science fiction tales that involve death rays, it probably isn't surprising that many people assume that the laser's most important function in the future will be as a weapon. In reality, the development of lasers for this purpose has been insignificant. Although the kind of heat that lasers can produce is capable of totally vaporizing matter, they have proven to be far too expensive to use as individual weapons and have shown no important advantages over other weapons.

Recently, lasers have also been suggested as a means of defense against a nuclear attack. In 1984, the United States unveiled its Strategic Defense Initiative, which calls for satellites to be armed with a battery of laser weapons that would destroy missiles before they could strike their target. Enormous obstacles, however, such as an estimated cost of $1 trillion stand in the way of such a defense system.

The use of the laser as part of a space-age arsenal is not as promising as the possibilities the instrument has opened up in other areas. So far, the medical world has just tapped the surface of laser treatment. Lasers are being tested for their effectiveness in everything from fusing cavities and removing birthmarks to fighting cancer, treating paralysis, and restoring fertility.

As concerns grow about the dwindling supply of energy sources such as coal, and the safety problems that plague present nuclear power reactors, nuclear fusion may be our best future power source. Mind-boggling temperatures are required to unleash the tremendous amount of energy that would result from the fusion or joining of atoms. Without the discovery of lasers, scientists would have no hope of ever achieving the estimated 100,000,000° C flashes of heat necessary to bring about a fusion reaction. Advances in laser technology may one day be the key to an unlimited supply of energy through nuclear fusion that would be far safer than today's nuclear power.

The credit for opening the way for lasers to make their impact on the world must be shared by a host of people. But in the opinion of the Nobel committee, Charles Hard Townes was most responsible. For his contributions, Townes was honored—along with Russian maser researchers Nikolai Basov and Alexander Prokhorov—with the Nobel Prize for physics in 1964.

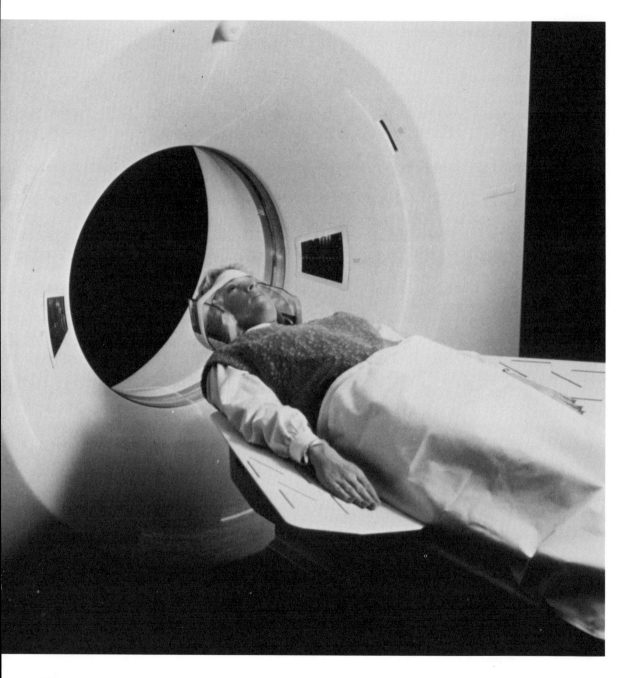

8

The CT Scanner: 3-D Pictures of the Brain

We've seen how Roentgen's X rays gave the medical world a window through the skin and how Einthoven's electrocardiograph tapped into electronic messages being sent by the heart. But even these great inventions still left the toughest territory of all to explore: the brain. This master control center, which governs all the functions of the body, is so important and so delicate that nature encased it in the sturdy protective armor of the skull. But while the skull provides an effective barrier against outside forces, it also keeps vital information about the health

A CT scanner takes a three-dimensional picture of a patient's brain.

of the brain sealed inside. Until the development of the CT – or CAT – scanner in the 1970s, any thorough probe of the brain was difficult, painful, and very dangerous.

A classic example of how Nobel inventions are often stepping-stones toward new technology, CT scanners would not have been possible without two Nobel-honored inventions: the transistor, which led to great improvements in computers, and X-ray photography. But unlike many modern inventions, the CT scanner did not take many years and countless scientists and technicians to develop. Instead, the idea for, and execution of, this machine were masterminded by Godfrey Hounsfield, a throwback to the tradition of the basement workshop inventor.

Hounsfield's Brainstorm

Hounsfield, who was born in Newark, England, in 1919, was more comfortable getting his hands dirty in a machine shop than he was working out the abstract mathematical problems usually associated with an inventor. As a youngster living on a farm, he was constantly tinkering with machinery and by age 13 had constructed a record player from spare parts.

Unlike nearly every other modern Nobel Prize winner in a technical field, Hounsfield never earned a Ph.D., nor does he have a long list of academic credits. His higher education consisted of a stint studying radiocommunications at City and Guilds College in London and course work in electrical and mechanical engineering at Faraday House Electrical Engineering College. But the man is a wizard in any kind of mechanical, high-technology field. During World War II, he developed radar systems and later worked as a computer designer and project engineer on the first large solid-state computer manufactured in England.

Hounsfield's success was partially due to his fearlessness in trying out strange, new ideas even though, as he once admitted, "ninety-nine percent of them turn out to be rubbish." By 1967, the new generation of computers had become so advanced that they were ready to be put to some extraordinary uses. Since computers were able to recognize shapes in the form of printed letters, Hounsfield wondered if they could also recognize and piece together more elaborate images. He speculated that if a large number of X-ray or gamma-ray (radiation with shorter wavelengths than X rays) photographs were taken of the brain one slice at a time and then sent to a computer, the computer would be able to construct a three-dimensional picture of the brain's internal structure.

Encouraged by the British Ministry of Health, Hounsfield wasted no time in showing that *this* idea was not rubbish. Although he was not a mathematician and was unaware of the computations made by United States physicist Allan Cormack, who had spelled out how such a machine would function, Hounsfield worked his way through problems by trial and error. By the end of 1968, he had constructed his first laboratory model of a CT scanner. (The letters *CT* stand for computerized tomography, which, in simpler terms, means a computerized cross-sectional slice.) Hounsfield's first effort used gamma rays, but he quickly switched to the safer X rays.

By 1971, the first CT scanner was installed at Atkinson Morley Hospital in London. The equipment consisted of four parts: a generator, a scanning unit, a computer, and a viewing unit. The generator provided the X rays for use in scanning. The scanning unit, which consisted of an X-ray source and a detector, was housed in a chamber that surrounded the patient's

Godfrey Hounsfield is pictured with his Nobel Prize-winning invention.

head. The unit rotated one degree at a time around the head while the source sent out a narrow beam of X rays that scanned rapidly over the brain. The detector recorded over 28,000 readings while moving a full 180 degrees. This information was sent to a computer, which combined readings from all angles to create a three-dimensional picture of the brain and displayed it on the viewing unit.

From Suspicion to Acceptance

As with most new inventions, CT scanners were greeted by some observers with suspicion and scorn. As more and more hospitals began to order them in the 1970s, cost-conscious consumer groups blasted CT scanners as being nothing but expensive playthings for doctors. In fact, the machines *were* expensive, running

United States physicist Allan Cormack shared Hounsfield's 1979 Nobel Prize.

about $300,000 for the first ones and inflating in cost to over $1 million by the 1980s. But in 1979, the Nobel committee came to the defense of CT scanners by awarding its prize for physiology or medicine to Godfrey Hounsfield and Allan Cormack. Other medical experts endorsed the machine, declaring that it was the most revolutionary development in radiology since Roentgen's X rays.

A CT scan is a vast improvement over an ordinary X ray. Whereas an X ray produces clear results only in areas where the differences in tissue density are great, CT scanners can distinguish between soft tissues that are within 0.5 percent of the same density. The clarity of a CT scanner display is 100 times sharper than that of an X-ray photograph. Whereas an X ray cannot always distinguish between a blood clot and a tumor in a stroke victim, a CT scan can provide a clear picture of the difference. The procedure is also safer than a normal brain X ray because it uses such a narrow beam of X rays.

CT scanning is so simple and harmless that it is considered an outpatient treatment. The entire operation can be done in just a few minutes with no special preparation, and the patient can get up and leave immediately after. The CT scanner easily pays back its cost by painlessly diagnosing the causes of seizures, strokes, dementia (loss of intellectual functions), and severe dizziness and fevers—taking the place of some excruciatingly painful and dangerous procedures. One of the worst of these was pneumoencephalography, which was formerly used to locate tumors in the brain. It involved the displacing of cranial fluid with air to provide enough of a contrast so that differences in brain tissue would show up on an X-ray screen. CT scans have also reduced the number of exploratory brain surgeries that have to be performed.

One of the most promising uses of the CT scanner is in the monitoring of osteoporosis—a disease characterized by spinal fractures caused by the loss of minerals in the bone that affects large numbers of older women. A timely CT scan can

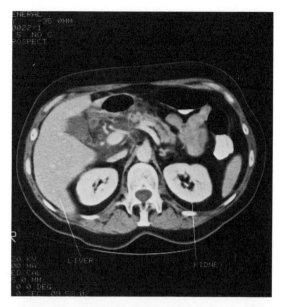

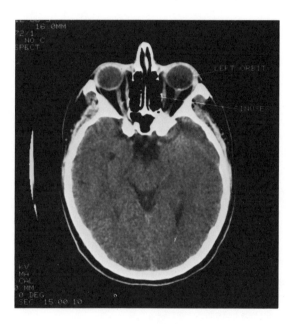

These CT scans show detailed cross-sections of the human abdomen (top), head (left), and spine (bottom).

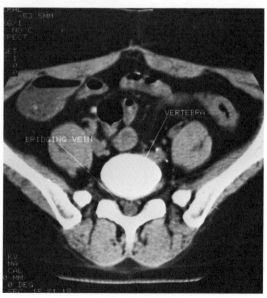

73

identify women with dangerously low mineral levels in their spines so the condition can be corrected before it is too late. The CT scanner's ability to detect minor abnormalities of the brain has also helped in the study of the disease anorexia nervosa, showing that the eating disorder can cause brain damage and may lead to permanent mental impairment.

As usual, this Nobel-honored invention has been adapted to uses far beyond what was originally intended. The medical world now has CT scanners that take three-dimensional pictures of the internal structures of the entire body. This painlessly eliminates the need for such dreaded methods of diagnosis as catheters (tiny tubes threaded into blood vessels and tracked through the body) and dye injections used to increase the clarity of X rays—methods that can in themselves cause strokes or heart attacks, or kidney damage in diabetics. Thanks to Hounsfield's ingenious thinking, doctors can use CT scans to get "road maps" of internal organs and systems and use that knowledge to fight diseases and malfunctions all over the body.

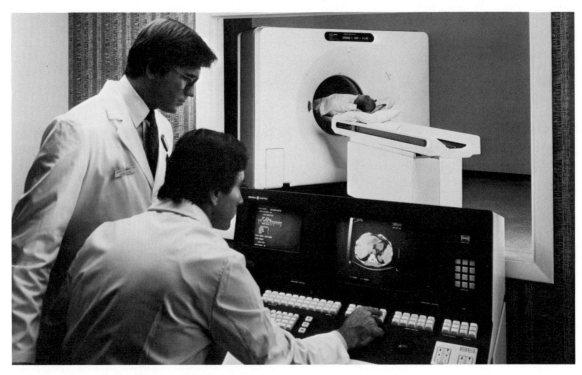

Doctors study a CT scan of a patient's abdomen.

Glossary

amplify — increase the strength of a signal

atoms — the tiny building blocks of the chemical elements

coherent light — light waves that travel in the same direction and frequency

conduct — to allow the passage of electricity

cosmic rays — streams of tiny, high-energy particles that bombard the gases of the earth's upper atmosphere

current — a flow of electricity

electrode — a conductor that a current entering or leaving an electronic device flows through

electromagnetic waves — waves of electric and magnetic force, including gamma rays, X rays, ultraviolet light, visible light, infrared light, and radio waves

electrons — negatively charged particles that rapidly orbit the nucleus of an atom

frequency — the number of waves that pass a certain point per second

half-life — the time it takes for half of the atoms of a radioactive substance to disintegrate

incoherent light — light waves that travel in different directions and frequencies

intensity — brightness of light

interfere — collide, as with waves

magnetic field — an area of force that forms in the space around anything that is magnetic or carries an electric current.

mass number — the sum of the protons and neutrons in an atom

neutrons — tiny particles that, along with protons, make up the nucleus of most atoms

nucleus — the core of an atom, usually composed of protons and neutrons

phase change — a shift in the times that a wave reaches its highest and lowest points

photon — a tiny bundle of radiant energy such as light

protons — positively charged particles that, along with neutrons, make up a nucleus

radiation — a form of energy, such as electromagnetic waves and nuclear radiation, that is given off in waves or particles

radioactive — giving off energy by the disintegration of the nucleus

receiver — the portion of communication equipment by which a message is received

rectify — allow electric current to travel in only one direction at a time

semiconductor — a material that conducts electricity better than an insulator, which blocks current, but not as well as a metal, which allows electricity to flow freely

signal — the sound or image conveyed by communication equipment

spontaneous emission — the random release of excess energy from an excited atom in the form of a photon, or particle of light

stimulated emission — the controlled release of excess energy in the form of a photon, or particle of light, that triggers an excited atom to release a photon

transmitter — the portion of communication equipment by which a message is sent

vacuum tube — a tube-like device used to control electric current

wavelength — the distance between a certain point on one wave and a comparable point on the next wave

Index

(Numbers in bold face refer to photographs)

77

ABOUT THE AUTHOR

Nathan Aaseng, who grew up in suburban Minneapolis, Minnesota, is a widely published author of books for young readers. He has explored far-ranging areas of interest, with college majors in English and biology, and work experience as a microbiologist/biochemist. Now a full-time writer, Aaseng has continued to delve into diverse subjects and has had more than 50 books published in the areas of sports strategy, biography, inspiration, and fiction. He now lives in Eau Claire, Wisconsin, with his wife and four children.

ACKNOWLEDGMENTS:
The photographs in this book are reproduced through the courtesy of: pp. 6, 8, 9, 38, 56, 60, 71, 72, the Nobel Foundation; pp. 11, 15, 16, 28, 30, National Library of Medicine; pp. 12, 13, 29, 68, Mayo Clinic; pp. 14, 20, 21, 23, 48, Library of Congress; pp. 18, 24, 25 (bottom), Minnesota Historical Society; p. 25 (top), *St. Paul Daily News* and Minnesota Historical Society; p. 26, University of Minnesota Archives; p. 31, American Heart Association; p. 32, Graphic Controls Corporation; p. 34, Prof. H. Festenstein, Dept. of Immunology, London Hospital Medical College, London, UK; p. 40 (left), Interferon Sciences, Inc.; p. 40 (right), Hybritech Incorporated; p. 41, American Medical Association; pp. 43, 50, Control Data; pp. 44, 45, 46, 47, 49, 63, AT&T Bell Laboratories; p. 52, Mexican National Tourist Council; p. 58, Brad Nelson; p. 62, Columbia University; p. 65, Laser Materials Processing, Inc.; p. 66, Brian Quintard, Laser Institute of America; pp. 73, 74, General Electric. Back cover photograph courtesy of the Nobel Foundation. Cover art by Mark Wilken.